Elemental Friends

Written & Illustrated by

Janet Crosby

ISBN 978-1-7389406-2-2
Library and Archives Canada
06/10/2024

Friends

To one who first did plant the seed,
So now these tales we all may read.

One who did proofread and edit,
Sincerely deserves a lot of credit.

One who helped with layout and design,
I'm exceedingly grateful for her time.

She who gifted sentences that hook,
Greatly enriching every book.

To all my family and friends who wished me well,
I'm more grateful to you than words can tell.

Each know who you are,
To me a brightly shining star.

Elemental Friends Contents

Introducing the Elementals

Elementals are associated with an element of nature

such as earth, wind, water or fire.

The Elementals in this book are Fairies, Sprites, Dwarfs

Elves, Gnomes and Trolls.

They are associated with the element of earth.

They are also known as the Wee Folk.

Fairies have wings and some have snouts.

Sprites are insect-like fairies.

Dwarfs are short and stocky.

Elves are tall, slim, usually attractive, with very large ears.

Gnomes are tiny and thin, with very long noses.

Trolls vary in appearance. Some are homely, ogre-like

giants with large noses.

The Insect-Like Sprite
Janet Crosby

The Insect-Like Sprite

Deep in the land of the insect-like sprite,
Everything's blissful, yellow and bright.

Elementals gather to see them at play,
'Cause sprites are so cheerfully happy all day.

They race and they twirl as they zip on by,
Bringing joy, as they flit, frolic and fly.

Snout fairy, trolls, dwarfs are a-twitter,
And merrily watch with eyes all a-glitter.

Sprites are so giving, loving and kind,
They bring comfort and peace to many a mind.

Sprites, being wise, intuitively know,
They can heal elementals of their troubles and woe.

So, with each wee folk they pause at an ear,
To whisper a kindness they're needing to hear.

One after another, they continue this way,
An encouraging word to thoughtfully say.

Simply be brave and never give up,
Count your blessings, see a full cup.

You are enough, believe in it, too,
I love spending this fun time with you.

You are loved, this is true.
Be happy, shine and simply be you.

You're a joy to be around.
The very best friend I've ever found.

Thoughtful, kind and amazing!
You deserve a lot of praising.

You make me so very proud,
I'd like to shout it right out loud!

On and on and on this goes,
Till all the wee folk have no woes.

As the sun sets on the gathering,
Sprites will pause with all their flattering.

Then elementals feeling deeply gifted,
Will journey home, their spirits lifted.

An Elemental Reflection

We can all benefit from the kind words of a friend.

Janet Crosby
The Wee Folk Meet the Standing-Frogs

The Wee Folk Meet the Standing-Frogs

The time the wee folk met the frogs,
They'd journeyed to the land of bogs.

Deming Dwarf, he knew the place
The standing-frogs were known to grace.

They'd travelled since the sun was up,
Barely having time to sup.

Finally, the pond came into view,
Which created quite the hullabaloo!

Its color was both blue and grey,
Tall grasses round did swish and sway.

Flowering lily pads were scattered,
O'er the water's surface gathered.

Bullrushes rose tall, brown and soft,
Birds were flying high aloft.

Many creatures' voices sounded,
Making the wee folk feel surrounded.

Chirping, crying, croaking, cheeping,
A little bit of fear was creeping.

That scary creatures may be slinking,
And their trip could use re-thinking.

Deming Dwarf said, "You'll be alright,
There's not a thing amiss in plain sight.

Don't resort to dread and fear,
Let's just observe the creatures here.

Look, toads, turtles, tadpoles, too,
And then we've only named a few.

Crane, raccoon, mink, opossum,
I think this is truly awesome!

Duck, deer, dragonfly, heron,
Isn't it great, what we're sharing?

Beaver, blackbirds, bugs-on-water,
There's no extent what we'll discover.

Minnows, muskrats, moose and mole,
We may find their hidey hole!

Crickets, snails, crabs and owls,
Whoops, someone fell in, do we have any towels?"

Then surprising all and looking quite weird,
A standing-frog suddenly appeared.

It simply appeared without warning,
My, these frogs have been transforming.

Deming said, "Let's all stand right back,
Please be calm, no panic attack!

I know this frog, his name is Ribbit,
Let's be friendly, that's the spirit!

Dart Dwarf, please stop your shaking,
Frog Ribbits' character you're mistaking."

Then Dwarf Deming said, "Hello."
To which Ribbit replied, "Whistle, bark, croak and bellow."

All the wee folk then did cheer!
For a frog to speak is rare to hear.

None of course could understand,
Still, a talking-standing-frog, that's grand!

"See, there was nothing to be scared of,
We just had to show him our love.

Everything evolves, that's no crime,
You and I will change in our time,"

Said the wise-all-knowing Deming,
And he, my friends, is no mere lemming.

So, dear reader, you at some stage,

May see frogs who walk on two legs.

<u>An Elemental Reflection</u>

Friends come in all different shapes and sizes.

The Yellow Fairies
Janet Crosby

The Yellow Fairies

Down a winding, vine-like trail,
Meandering through both hill and dale,

Moving through different spaces,
Experiencing unseen places,

In the cheery month of mid-May,
Basking in its golden sun's ray,

Through an ever-changing spiral,
The likes of which there is no rival,

Taken on a dream-like journey,
Wondering what each turn may bring thee,

Then, at a narrow bend you're rounding,
You'll hear wee, tiny voices sounding.

Yes, tiny voices you will hear then,
Over there, in that sweet, fair glen.

From the trees you'll hear the sound,
The ones with tops, real big and round.

Wide and round are treetops standing,
As if the trees can't stop expanding.

Their trunks are rather short and stocky,
The landscape here is rich and rocky.

The sound you hear is lots of chatter,
Truthfully, it's mostly patter.

See, wee folk live within these trees,
Like a hive of busy, buzzing bees.

Yes, in the trees, they seem to crowd,
And when they do, it's very loud.

Ladders fill trees everywhere,
I'm not quite sure why they're there.

I suppose the ladders they could make
It easier than a branch to take?

So, many ladders have been placed,
To climb the trees with greater haste.

Yes, wee folk live within these trees,
Seemingly with grace and ease.

What they do up there, I've no thought,
Odds and ends, all sorts, what not?

Still, it seems a bit perplexing,
Yet perfectly suited to them, I'm guessing.

There are yellow fairies all around,
In the air, there on the ground.

Splendid and sublimely bright,
Friends of encouragement and of light!

Empowering to every fellow,
'Cause they are the color yellow.

Filling minds with beautiful thought and feeling,
How could that be unappealing?

Inspiring positivity and understanding,
The results of which are quite outstanding.

Fairy wisdom's what they're lending,
Elemental hearts are what they're mending.

All out enjoying one another,
Father, mother, sister, brother.

Family acquaintance, neighbor, friend,
Quality time we all could spend.

Getting out enjoying life,
Letting go of any strife.

Playing, laughing, music blaring,
Pairing, caring, kindly sharing.

Opening up our hearts real wide,

Even having that horsey ride!

An Elemental Reflection

Being positive lifts up our own spirits and we

attract a circle of happy friends.

Ole the Troll

Ole the Troll

Far off in a canyon, craggy and rough,
A troll awoke, both crabby and gruff.

He'd slept in a rocky canyon crevice,
Safe from danger, harm and menace.

Last night he'd found his bed of stone,
And lay there hidden, all alone.

He'd risen early from fitful slumber,
And from his crevice bed did lumber.

Still clumsy and heavy from his sleep,
Stomach gnawing for something to eat.

Ole gathered all his things together,
Donning his hat with its lovely feather.

Its wing of bird and raccoon tail,
That Ole had found along some trail.

Then, with sash and pouch secured most snugly,
Went down the boulder-ridden gully.

Towards the canyon floor and valley,
In search of food, he needed badly.

Perhaps some tubers, fruit or honey,
To satisfy his rumbling tummy.

Ole searched the valley and along the stream,
Where everything was lush and green.

But grumbled as his search grew broader,
Still nothing in his small pouch larder.

Then moments later, or not long after,
Ole heard the sound of distant laughter.

Of wee folk above that knoll over there,
Wouldn't it be nice to talk and share?

So up and over that steepish knoll,
Appeared the head of Ole-the-Troll.

And dwarfs exchanging friendly banter,
Ran off as fast as horses canter.

But Ole was tall, his stride was wide,
And soon the troll was by their side.

He scooped some up and had them trapped,
Within his arms and long nails wrapped.

Other dwarfs ran for their life,
Hearts pumping fast with fear and strife.

Ole's voice boomed, "What's the trouble?
Why are you running on the double?"

One dwarf spoke up with courage and grit,
"Stop, Mr. Troll, we don't like this one bit.

First you come here acting surly and mean,
Terrifying us all and causing a scene.

Also, you are most contrary,
Truthfully, you're very scary.

You have my friends there gripped with fear,
Your reason being not yet clear.

Your attitude is not polite,
And you've given everyone a fright!"

To which Ole-the-Troll replied sadly,
Realizing now, he'd acted badly,

"Well, it's just that I've been bored and lonely,
I personally think, its cause I'm homely.

You all seemed to be having so much fun,
It made me want to have me some."

Ah! It seemed the troll endured some hardship,
So, the wee folk offered him their friendship.

To that Ole replied, "Yes! Okay!
And also, wee folk, by the way,

Aside from feeling down and blue,

I'm also very hungry too."

To which brave dwarf replied on cue,

"We have dead rodents, will that do?"

<u>An Elemental Reflection</u>

You catch more bees with honey than you do with vinegar.

Little Mervyn Melrose Magnusson
Janet Crosby

Little Mervyn Melrose Magnusson

Little Mervyn Melrose Magnusson,

Was a human boy with siblings none.

Mervyn Melrose spent most days,

Embellishing tales and making waves.

All this was done, I should mention,

As an attempt to get his folks' attention.

It'd be nice to have a friend or two,

Still, it did no good to sit and stew.

Yes, he could sit at home and moan,
Or, get creative on his own.

There was plenty to do outside his door,
Acres of farmland to explore.

Fields of corn and crops of clover,
Many cool animals in their enclosure.

Cow and pig, sheep and horse,
He could always speak with them, of course.

There's a lovely stream with chub and trout,
Where he could go and mess about.

Or, play in his fort in the copse of pine,
An awesome place to spend some time.

So, having decided, he gathered his pole,
And off towards the stream did stroll.

He passed through fields of grasses dancing,
Where horses sewing oats were prancing.

With each step, grasshoppers leaping,
Awoken while on grasses sleeping.

Dragonflies were quickly flitting,
Forward, backward, sometimes sitting.

He noticed caterpillars munching,

Upon some milkweed plants were lunching.

A chrysalis would soon be forming,

A monarch butterfly transforming.

As he continued with his walking,

He heard many noisy grackles squawking.

Crow and blue jay were also calling,

While in the grass some snake was crawling.

Where the landscape became rough and sloping,

Bullfrogs were heard loudly croaking.

Mervyn would have to watch his step,
On this part of his fishing trek.

Best not to hurry, force or rush,
As he maneuvered through dense trees and brush.

But, as he made his way, he stumbled,
Lost his balance, and did tumble.

Perhaps loose ground had caused a slip,
Or, on a tree root, he did trip.

'Cause down he went, his footing losing,
Probably, his body bruising.

He lay there motionless, unmoving,
Flat on his back, like he was snoozing.

While Mervyn lay there on the ground,
Many wee folk gathered round.

It seemed to them he may be dead!
But Mervyn had simply bumped his head.

The wee folk looked on, curiously peering,
Their concern for Mervyn, quite endearing.

Mervyn remained silent, but aware,
Of the elves and dwarfs around him there.

Remaining still, one eye slightly open,

This wasn't a dream he was hopin.

Lying there he made no sound,

Thinking, could these be friends I have found?

'Cause from where he lay, he could see,

They were as cool and cheerful as could be.

So, Mervyn determined in the end,

To make each one his special friend.

An Elemental Reflection

Imaginary friends are a normal and healthy

part of childhood play.

Bluebird Birdie Bird

Bluebird Birdie Bird

Durward had proposed to Phrania Fairy,

Promising to find them a home before they'd marry.

To accompany him on this quest,

Of finding his bride the perfect nest,

Was his treasured, feathered friend Birdie,

'Cause the homes he built were safe and sturdy.

They departed in the hush of early morning,

'Fore the sun would find their valley warming.

He'd said farewell at Phrania's favorite spot,
His heart real full and his stomach taut.

He would never forget 'fore he turned his back
The way she'd looked as there she sat,

Amongst the pretty, purple periwinkle,
Her rosy red cheeks all a-dimple, her sparkling, emerald eyes a-twinkle.

Now the two friends had set about,
Searching their elemental lands throughout.

Durward earnestly combing the landscape o'er,
Including every nook and cranny of the forest floor.

While Birdie circled from above,
Determined to find that place his friend would love.

He'd call down what he thought was a good suggestion,
Yet Durward would reply, "That's out of the question."

"Like, why not up here on this high mountain peak?"
"Too far to climb, with small legs and feet."

"Or, look, I've found an eagle's nest."
Thinking, wouldn't Durward be impressed?

Rather, he'd say, "Birdie, I have a strong hunch,
An eagle or two may have us for lunch."

"Right! How about this lush forest swamp?
Plenty of room for a family to romp."

"Birdie, I've heard there is a hungry gator,
I'd rather not die sooner than later."

They'd searched until day had come to its end,
when Durward called up to his bluebird friend,

"Birdie, I'm tired and in much need of a bite,
Let's say we quit and rest for the night."

"Okay," said Birdie, catching some vile-looking bugs,
Some berries, some insects and one or two slugs.

While below, Durward labored constructing his bed,
Gathering leaves, twigs and some fluff for his head.

Later, each settled down tired from their chores,
The evening soon filling with Durward's soft snores.

While Birdie slept soundly in a very tall fir,
His head nestled snugly in his feather coiffeur.

Early next morning Durward woke with a squeak,
When Birdie roused him with the point of his beak.

"Wake up, Durward, and let us make haste,
I've found you a home; no time to waste."

"Birdie, it's a pair of human shoes!
Lucky for me they come in twos.

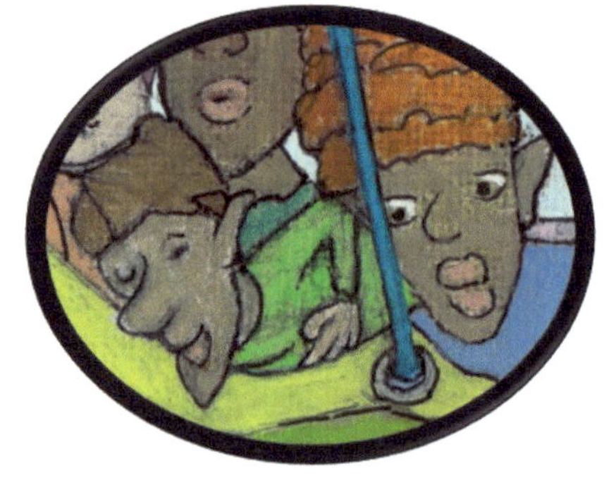

'Cause Nana and Papa can live here, too,
Right next door in the other shoe!

It's the perfect home, I must admit,
For our whole family, a perfect fit."

"Durward, I prefer the top of a mountain or pine,
But I realize they're too tall for you to climb.

I know those places are much too high,
'Cause unlike me you cannot fly.

So, I'll build my nest, if it's fine with you,

On the branch beside your home, a shoe.

We may be friends of a different feather,

Still best friends like us should stick together."

All felt on top of the world in the end,

Including Bluebird Birdie Bird, his very best friend.

__An Elemental Reflection__

Compromise is valuable in creating harmony between friends.

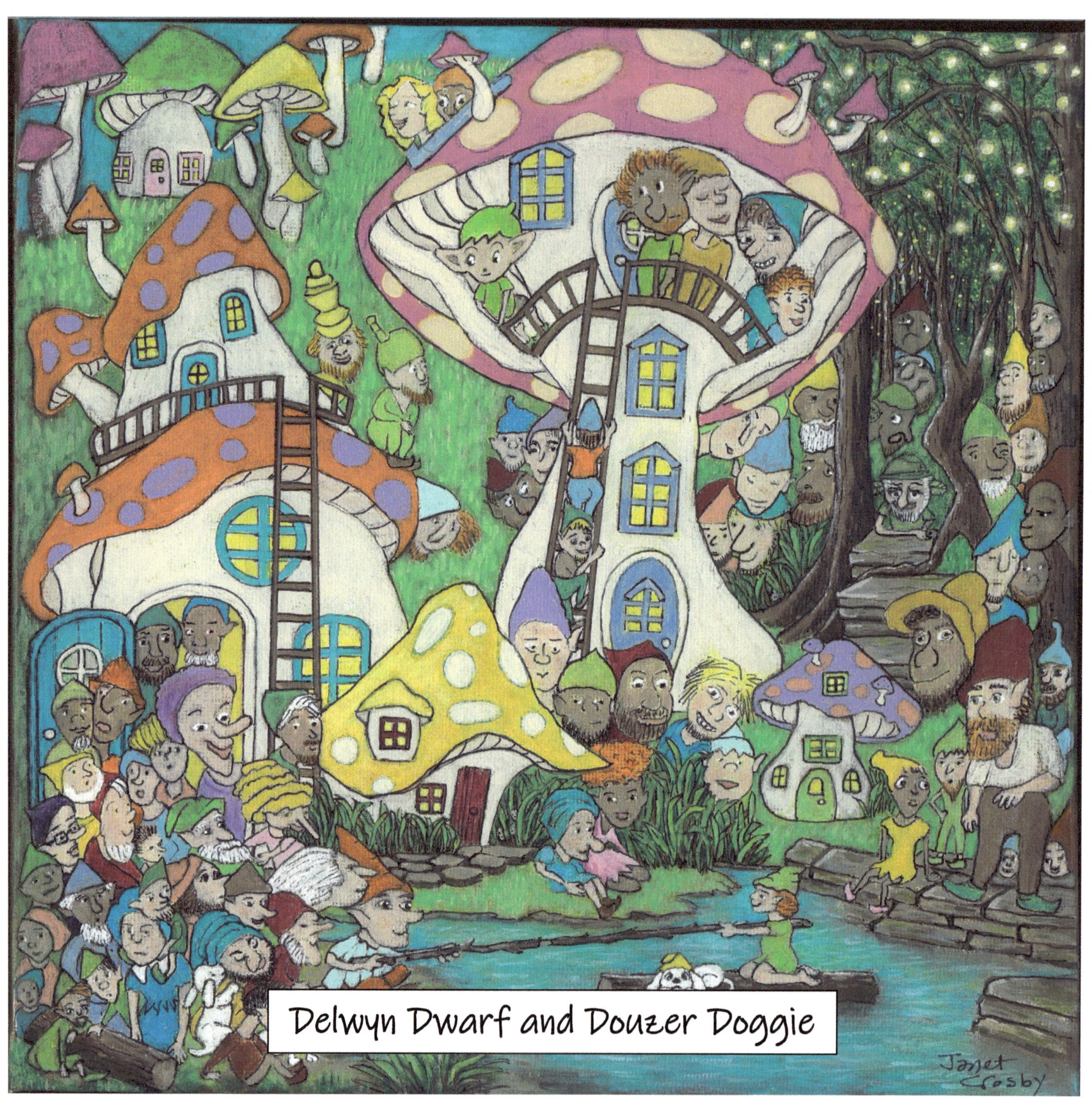

Delwyn Dwarf and Douzer Doggie
Janet Crosby

Delwyn Dwarf and Douzer Doggie

There's a land where mushrooms grow as homes,

For fairies, dwarfs, elves and gnomes.

It's down a narrow, hidden trail,

And found by searching hill and vale.

Through the tangle and bramble of dense, wooden growth,

Some prickly and spiny, truthfully both.

Past thickets all briery, bristly and burred,

Certainly not a journey preferred.

But if you're determined, persevere and prevail,
I'm sure you'll succeed in finding the trail.

At the doorway, fairy lights fill the skies,
Like a host of bright-lit fireflies.

At the entryway, they glint, gleam and glow,
As their beacons of light they bestow,

Illuminating your way to that magical land,
Where mushroom-like houses there do stand.

Here the sky is a beautiful, turquoise-blue,
With mushroom houses of every hue.

Some are large and others tall,
Perfectly suiting elementals all.

While others, still growing from a smallish home,
Are large enough for fairy and gnome.

The community is buzzing, all busy and bustling,
While Delwyn Dwarf and his dog sit nuzzling,

Likely pondering some trouble they may stir up,
As mischievousness appeals to boy and pup.

Delwyn, having an extreme zest for life,
Causes his parents many moments of strife.

His tricks and games he seldom stops,
Like playing hide-n-seek in mushroom tops,

Refusing to come out when mom calls her son,
He really can be the naughty one.

Delwyn, oblivious to why Mom gets in a tizzy,
Sees his escapades as harmless ways to keep busy

Douzer Doggie, who simply loves being with him,
Tags along happily with vigor and vim.

Delwyn delights in dressing Douzer up as an elf,
Douzer, indifferent, lets Delwyn enjoy himself.

The two get lost together quite a lot,
Those episodes, for his parents, panic brought.

Like the time they roamed off the fairy path,
Resulting in his parent's wrath.

Yes, he was often in some sort of mess,
His folks voiced their concern, their love, their stress.

Delwyn would reply, "Sorry, it won't happen again,"
Small head down and an impish grin.

No surprise, new ideas constantly formed in his mind,
Leading him into his very next bind.

"Douzer, we're going sailing today on the lake,
We simply have a raft to make.

Actually, it's going to be this log.
I'm a small boy and you're only one dog.

Yes, this should fit us like a charm,
Can't see us coming to any harm."

With the plan in place, the log was pushed in,
Delwyn never considering neither could swim.

The two floated around, content for a bit,
Soon becoming bored with nowt to do but sit.

Delwyn began fearing into deep water they'd fall,
Surmising sailing a log wasn't so much fun after all,

For Douzer's sake he tried to be brave,
Hoping someone soon their lives would save.

"Douzer, my friend, we should soon be ashore,
Then something exciting and new we'll explore.

My folks will certainly miss us both soon,

Afterall, it's surely nearly noon."

An Elemental Reflection

A dog can be an unconditionally loving companion and friend.